PROJECT 2025

KEEP YOUR
LAWS OFF

Project 2025

An Authoritarian Takeover of the United States

By J. L. Wertis

Published by Bequille Publishing
Tulsa, Oklahoma, 74137

Frontispiece photo by Gayatri Malhotra, *Unspash.com*
Afterword photo by Colin Lloyd, *Unsplash.com*

ISBN: 978-1-7364326-6-2

First Edition

COPYRIGHT AND DISTRIBUTION

This is a work of non-fiction. No names were changed, no characters created and no events fabricated. Any events referenced are real, drawn from a variety of sources. Statements presented have been researched, fact-checked, and verified.

Historical references, and statements about social, psychological and philosophical subjects were researched against respected published works on the subject. The Author does not assume and hereby disclaims any liability, to any party, for errors or omissions, whatever the cause.

Also by J. L. WERTIS

THE LONGEST FOUR YEARS: The Trump Administration's Assault on Democracy, and the Rise of White Nationalism

ALTERNATE REALITY: The Ultimate Guide to the Mad, Mad World of Conspiracy Theories

***LIES, CRIMES AND OTHER POLITICAL SKULLDUGGERY*:** The Informed Voters Guide to Political Terms, Concepts and Claims Heard on the News

Combinations or associations...may now and then answer popular ends and...become potent engines, by which cunning, ambitious, and unprincipled men will be enabled to subvert the power of the people and to usurp for themselves the reins of government, destroying afterwards the very engines which have lifted them to unjust dominion.

~George Washington
1796 Farewell Address

TABLE OF CONTENTS

We the people are the rightful masters of both Congress and the courts, not to overthrow the Constitution but to overthrow the men who pervert the Constitution.

~Abraham Lincoln

INTRODUCTION

Project 2025 is a 922-page document, crafted by the Heritage Foundation, that seeks to radically alter the structure and function of the American government by (in their own words) *"dismantling the administrative state"* through what many have called an authoritarian takeover of the United States. It bills itself as a policy agenda—*"a 180-day playbook to be implemented beginning on day one by the next Republican president"*—presumed to be Donald Trump.

The contributors to Project 2025 tend to be white, ultra-conservative, Fundamentalist Christian Nationalists—many of whom have backgrounds with conspiracy theorist organizations, and/or have racist or anti-sematic histories.

It was clear from the very first paragraph that this was not going to be an easy read. The proliferation of political diatribe, misinformation, obvious bias, racism, and plain ignorance of some of the authors, was frustrating, overwhelming and frankly exhausting.

Parts of it read like something written in the 1800s before medical science had advanced beyond blood-letting, humours, and trepanning (the process of boring a hole into somebody's skull).

Other parts took me back to the 50's and 60's when women had few rights, were subservient to men, had no voice in government, and were expected to be "barefoot, pregnant, and in the kitchen" with dinner and a drink waiting when their spouse came home.

Yes, I read the ENTIRE DOCUMENT, although not in front-to-back order. With a document more than 900 pages long, having a PDF download made it much easier to do word and phrase searches to substantiate (or disprove) the claims I had been seeing on social media.

The more I read, the more it became clear what the underlying goals of Project 2025 are:

> (1) Establish a governmental structure where <u>ultimate unchecked power</u> resides in the Executive Branch.
>
> (2) Give the President direct supervision of the Office of Personnel Management (OPM) to ensure that all government employees are loyal to the President and his/her agenda.
>
> (3) Remove the requirement for Congressional approval to enact laws or policies (eliminate the balance of power).

(4) Install a judicial system that supports and will enforce Fundamentalist Christian ideology, incorporating biblical literalism, biblical infallibility and biblical inerrancy into legal decisions and legislation regarding education, science, medicine, sex, climate, the role of women (subservient to men); and the *"natural superiority of the white race."*

(5) Weaponize the Department of Justice to enact retribution against dissenters, punish disloyalty, and eliminate political opposition through arrest, incarceration, or other punishments up to and including execution.

(6) Gut the FBI, eliminating the Office of General Counsel, (approximately 300 attorneys), Office of Legislative Affairs, and Office of Public Affairs along with any other offices that can be eliminated without Congressional approval.

(7) Abandon the current Globalist policy by immediately pulling out of international organizations that don't serve the administration's interests, cancelling all commitments and alliances.

(8) Adopt an "America First," Isolationist policy by immediately stopping the supply of weapons, money, and other military and humanitarian support to other nations; Close

> down military bases everywhere except those on American soil and bring all troops home.

Anyone who knows history will recognize the plan for what it is. The Project 2025 model is not a new idea. It has been implemented by other countries in the past with disastrous results.

In 1933 Germany, Hitler's ENABLING ACT gave him the authority to enact laws without parliamentary consent—effectively making the Reichstag (their equivalent of Congress) powerless. It dismantled democratic institutions and restructured government agencies to *align them with Hitler's goals* by eliminating officials and employees who refused to swear loyalty to Hitler. We all know how this turned out!

In the Soviet Union in 1929 Joseph Stalin declared himself dictator, centralizing power within the Communist Party by eliminating (both figuratively and actually) political opposition, *consolidating power within the executive branch.* He weaponized what was the equivalent of our Dept of Justice to arrest, jail, and punish dissenters. Like Hitler, he restructured the various agencies to align with his interests. This absolute power resulted in what was known as the "GREAT PURGE." To eliminate those who objected to the Communist Party, he ordered massive executions from 1936 to 1938. Some estimates put the number at about 750,000 with an additional million or more sent to forced labor camps, known as Gulags.

Introduction

The People's Republic of China under Mao Zedong in 1966 used the same basic plan to establish the Communist Party's GREAT PROLETARIAN CULTURAL REVOLUTION. Its stated goal was to "purge" remnants of capitalist and traditional elements from Chinese society. They began by restructuring the institutions of government to align them with communist ideology—targeting "disloyal" government officials and party members. Mao's unchecked authority led to implementation of extremist policies resulting in devastating economic disaster and widespread famine.

Present day Russia is an example of how a government like this looks, and where the U.S. is headed under Project 2025.

Democracy cannot succeed unless those who express their choice are prepared to choose wisely. The real safeguard of democracy, therefore, is education.

~Franklin D. Roosevelt

The Heritage Foundation

The Heritage Foundation, founded in 1973, is an activist American ultra-conservative think tank based in Washington, D.C. that many former Republican presidents, including Ronald Reagan, had consulted regarding policy initiatives. Many of Reagan's policies were taken from Heritage Foundation studies, including its Mandate for Leadership. The Heritage Foundation has had significant influence in U.S. public policy-making since its inception, and was at one time considered a centrist voice for the Republican party. It was well-respected in the political policy arena by members of both parties.

Unfortunately, the Foundation took a hard right turn in December 2012 when Jim DeMint, a U.S. Senator from South Carolina, took over to lead the Foundation. He implemented changes that reversed the principles, standards, and direction the Foundation had held for years. In response to DeMint's new practice, several scholars at the Foundation quit.

Currently, seven of the organizations on Project 2025's Advisory Board have been designated as extremist or hate groups by the Southern Poverty Law Center.

In 2013, a Heritage Foundation study about immigration reform, co-authored by Jason Richwine and Robert Rector, was widely criticized across the political spectrum for its methodology and because of Richwine's 2009 doctoral dissertation alleging that Hispanics and Blacks are intellectually inferior to Whites and have trouble assimilating because of a supposed genetic predisposition to lower IQ, and that immigrants' IQs should be considered when crafting public policy. Jason Richwine, under pressure, resigned his position in May of 2013.

In June 2015, Donald Trump announced his candidacy for the 2016 Republican presidential nomination. The Heritage Foundation was not a fan. The following month the leader of Heritage Action, appeared on a Fox News panel, stating, *"Donald Trump's a clown. He needs to be out of the race."*

In August, Stephen Moore, a Heritage Foundation economic writer, stated, regarding Trump's policy positions, *"the problem for Trump is that he's full of all of these contradictions. He's kind of a tabula rasa (air head) on policy."*

In December, Heritage executive vice president Kim

Holmes, spoke out in opposition to Trump's candidacy, stating *"Trump is not a conservative."* He also criticized Trump supporters as *"behaving more like an alienated class of Marxist imagination than as social agents of stability and tradition. They are indeed thinking like revolutionaries, only now their ire is aimed at their progressive masters and the institutions they control."*

In May 2017, the Foundation's board of trustees voted unanimously to terminate DeMint as its president. DeMint's firing was praised by some, including former Congressman Mickey Edwards (R-OK), who said he saw it as *"a step by the Foundation to pare back its partisan edge and restore its reputation as a pioneering think tank."*

In January 2018, Kay Coles James was ushered in as the Foundation's sixth president and the first African-American and first woman to hold that position. Roughly two years later, on March 22, 2021, she announced she was resigning from the Foundation.

In March 2021, former Vice President, Mike Pence authored and published an op-ed on the Heritage Foundation website making false claims of voter fraud in the 2020 presidential election, and numerous false claims about the For the People Act, a bill to expand voting rights. Facing criticism and corrections from multiple media outlets and fact-checking organizations, and disapproval from Heritage, Pence left the Foundation.

Kevin Roberts, a conservative Catholic, anti-abortion activist, and election denier became President of the Heritage Foundation in December 2021, ushering in the current Heritage Foundation policy of white Fundamentalist Christian Nationalism. Shortly after taking office, he established Project 2025—a plan to demolish the Constitutional structure of the federal government as established by the founding fathers, and consolidate power, including the Judicial Branch, in the office of the President, thereby, creating an unfettered autocracy.

In May of that same year, the Heritage Foundation completely reversed its position supporting military aid to Ukraine. In September, the Foundation's foreign policy director said the Foundation ordered him to retract his earlier statements supporting aid to Ukraine. He subsequently left the organization. In August 2023, Thomas Spoehr, the Foundation's Center for National Defense director, resigned his position over the policy changes.

The Heritage Foundation, a once staid, respected, conservative "think tank" devolved even further into white Fundamentalist Christian Nationalist extremism when Roberts took over.

In January 2024, Roberts confessed that he did not believe Joe Biden won the 2020 presidential election, and that he saw Heritage's role as *"institutionalizing Trumpism."*

Roberts has declared that he believed the recent Supreme Court decision made the President immune to prosecution and *"the way has been cleared for the second American Revolution, which will remain bloodless if the left allows it to be."* Following these claims on social media and on right-wing talk shows, Roberts has been described by some as *"a fascist, threatening the American people, with the newfound power of the president to kill people and pay no penalty."*

In a July 2024 broadcast on *Real America's Voice*, Roberts predicted that the *"second revolution"* would be complete by 2050, and that *"it will coincide with a new great awakening that will bring America to God."* Roberts further stated that *"God's law can, in fact, be a huge influence on the civil laws. Our definition of freedom is not the freedom to do whatever the heck we want, but the freedom to do what we ought"*—a vision for American government to function as *"the instrument through which God's wrath on evil is applied."*

Throughout Project 2025 a consistent theme emerges: the merging of an ultra-conservative agenda with white Fundamentalist Christian Nationalist theology.

Religious factions will go on imposing their will on others unless the decent people connected to them recognize that religion has no place in public policy. They must learn to make their views known without trying to make their views the only alternatives.

~Barry Goldwater
Former Republican U.S. House Member

Christian Nationalism

Often referred to as Christo-fascism, Fundamentalist Christian Nationalism primarily focuses on civil and criminal laws and legislation that reflect a strict view of Fundamentalist Christianity, establishing the role of Christian religion in political and social life as the exclusive moral and cultural guide, emphasizing biblical literalism. Fundamentalist Christians believe in biblical inerrancy and biblical infallibility including "young earth" creationism, a fiery hell, the virgin birth, Jesus's resurrection, the second coming, and the "Rapture."

By the end of the 20th century, the term Fundamentalist became synonymous with religious fanaticism or extremism, as adherence to Fundamentalist Christian beliefs was shown to have a high correlation with distrust and denial of science, from evolution to climate change to medical science. During the COVID-19 pandemic, Fundamentalist Christian Nationalists, convinced that God would protect them, opposed lockdowns, restrictions on social gatherings, and mask wearing that resulted in millions of deaths which they then attributed to "God's will."

At some point Fundamentalist Christian Nationalism stopped being solely about the faith and broadened to include what they refer to as "traditional American values"—something significantly less Biblically grounded and far more threatening to a democratic society.

They began demanding that certain movies be banned; dictating what books can and cannot be in libraries and schools; what subjects children can be taught in school—about sex/sexuality, American history, diversity, etc. This became even more dangerous to our democracy as they began to search for a political party or politician willing to introduce and support the passage of laws that aligned with their strict Fundamentalist Christian beliefs—laws that would force the rest of the country to live by their rules.

Although Jesus declared that his kingdom was *"not of this world"* and denounced advancing his kingdom through violence, many Fundamentalist Christians believe that America is God's Kingdom, the country's founding documents were *"divinely inspired,"* and only Christians are *"true Americans."* A prejudice towards minority groups framed around fear of *"the other"*—immigrants, racial, and sexual minorities—is based on their belief that Christianity *"celebrate[s] and privilege[s] the sacred history, liberty, and rightful rule of white conservatives."* They have become obsessed with the idea of forcing the country to live according to their standards and rules, and see this as a war where the ends justify the means—even to the point of violence.

Fundamentalist Christian Nationalism throughout history has been linked to political violence. A 2021 survey found that respondents who held Fundamentalist Christian Nationalist beliefs obtained their news from conspiratorial websites, QAnon posts, alt-right or white identity news sources such as FOX News, NewsMax, Breitbart News, etc. and right-wing talk radio. These same individuals exhibited increased approval of political violence.

The Fundamentalist faction of today's political right is the driving force behind the anti-abortion, anti-LGBTQ, and traditional family idea. Fundamentalists believe that women should be (by biblical mandate) subservient to men, should have as many children as possible, and should not work outside the home. Trump's Vice Presidential pick, J.D. Vance, has even expressed his belief that women should be forced to stay in abusive marriages, that no fault divorce should be abolished, and single and childless women should not have the right to vote *"because they have no stake in the future."*

Studies have found a close correlation between Fundamentalist Christian Nationalism and xenophobia, homophobia, misogyny, patriarchy, nativism, and restricting the civil rights of those unwilling to conform to their closely-held ideals of whiteness, citizenship, and male superiority.

The Fundamentalist Christian Nationalists in America are specifically targeting the LGBTQ community claiming that just by existing they are a *"danger to our family values and our children."* They typically use the terms "transgender ideology" and "sexualization of children" when talking about pornography, claiming that anything (or anyone) remotely resembling gay or transgender is pornographic. They go even further suggesting that *"telecommunications and technology firms that host pornography should be shut down, and any educators or public librarians who purvey porn should be classed as registered sex offenders."* Under their definition of pornography, sex education materials and materials or books that mention LGBTQ issues would be classified as pornographic and banned.

Fundamentalist Christian Nationalists have, in other countries, been willing to elect any impious, immoral, or irreligious head of state—"the devil himself"—as long as he supports their cause. This could explain how Trump became leader of a Fundamentalist Christian Nationalist movement.

Christian leaders from all around the country and the world are speaking out against Christian Nationalism and the threats it poses to the church, democracy and a nation's shared values.

What Is Project 2025?

Project 2025 is a 900+ page manifesto created by the Heritage Foundation over a number of years, titled: *PROJECT 2025: MANDATE FOR LEADERSHIP: A CONSERVATIVE PROMISE*, with an extremist agenda for a prospective second Trump term.

It's not really a plan as much as it is a Republican "fever dream." Unlike a true organization or business plan, it lacks substance, detail, and consistency from one chapter to the next. While there are some stated desired outcomes, there are few strategies outlined for achieving that outcome. There is no overall analysis as to how such a massive change would be managed while still having a fully operational government, or how it would impact the functioning of the government—either during the transition or following implementation—no measurable cost/benefit analysis, and no strategy for actual implementation. The Mission Statement for Project 2025 can be summed up as *"tear it all down and blame someone else if it turns out bad."*

THE TRUMP CONNECTION

Although Paul Dans, the Heritage Foundation staff member and Project 2025 director, was a former top adviser in the Trump administration, Trump has tried to distance himself from Project 2025 stating in a Truth Social post: *"I know nothing about Project 2025. I have no idea who is behind it."*

The following day he doubled down posting: *"I have not seen it, have no idea who is in charge of it, and, unlike our very well received Republican Platform, had nothing to do with it."*

In June, Dans appeared on Steve Bannon's *War Room* podcast declaring that Project 2025 was *"gonna be a D-Day invasion plan"* and urged listeners to *"flood the zone with us."* He further confirmed *"We're going to make this happen under President Trump. This is ultimately his direction and his team's direction;"* and that Project 2025 is *"systematically preparing to march into office and bring a new army, aligned, trained, and essentially weaponized conservatives ready to do battle."*

Trump himself is mentioned 311 times in the document. At least 66 Heritage Foundation employees and alumni were hired into the Trump administration and several hundred people from the Heritage database received jobs in the Trump government, including Betsy DeVos, Mick Mulvaney, Rick Perry, Scott Pruitt, Jeff Sessions, and others who became members of Trump's cabinet.

Analysts have described the plan as *"an authoritarian Christian Nationalist movement and a path for the United States to become an autocracy."* Several legal experts have expressed concerns that it would undermine the rule of law and destroy the separation of powers.

In March of 2024, the U.S. House Republican Study Committee (RSC) released its fiscal year 2025 budget proposal that closely echoes—some of it "word for word"—the agenda of Project 2025.

More than 200 former Trump Administration officials are involved with Project 2025. At least 31 of the 38 official authors and editors of Project 2025 have a connection to the former president. Some of his key allies and top former advisors are architects of the plan.

The Heritage Foundation itself proudly brags:

> *"the Trump administration embraced nearly two thirds of the 334 Heritage Foundation policy proposals presented to him during his last administration."*

In April 2022, Trump spoke at a Heritage Foundation dinner:

> *"This is a great group, and they're going to lay the groundwork and detail plans for exactly what our movement will do and what your movement will do when the American people give us a colossal mandate to save America."*

When Trump talks about becoming *"a dictator on day one,"* he's talking about Project 2025. When he says *"vote for me in 2024 and you'll never have to vote again,"* he's talking about Project 2025. When he tells you he will *"suspend the constitution,"* he's talking about Project 2025. When he says he will *"be your retribution,"* he's talking about Project 2025. When he says we should *"beat the f--- out" of the protesters,"* he's talking about Project 2025. He is intimately acquainted with Project 2025—he quotes it in nearly every one of his speeches.

In July 2024, Paul Dans stepped down amid intense criticism including from former president Trump. Dans is also leaving the Heritage Foundation. Representatives from Heritage Foundation explained that Project 2025 would be *"effectively ending its policy operations. However, efforts to build a conservative personnel apparatus will continue."*

Of course they are ending their policy operations. Project 2025 is finished and published. Now they are focused on identifying and training "conservative personnel" for implementation of Project 2025 should Trump or another extremist Republican be elected.

THE AUTHORITARIAN AGENDA

The following steps outline the scope of work laid out by Project 2025 for *"dismantling the administrative state"* and assuming total control over the United States Federal Government.

Ruth Ben-Ghiat, professor of history at NYU and author of the book *Strongman*, defines authoritarianism this way: *"It's when the executive branch and the leader find ways to take away checks and balances so they have a degree of power that they don't have in a democracy, and they find ways to take away the independence of the legislature and the independence of the judiciary. You need to get people to feel they have an existential threat facing them. And the more they feel uncertain and fearful, the more the strongmen can appear and say, 'I alone can fix it.'"*

This DEFINES what Project 2025 is about. Project 2025 proposes the dismantling of multiple independent agencies—including the Consumer Financial Protection

Bureau, the Transportation Security Administration (TSA), the Environmental Protection Agency (EPA), the Department of the Interior (DOI), Housing and Urban Development (HUD), the Department of Education (DOE), the Department of Homeland Security (DHS), and the National Oceanographic and Atmospheric Administration (NOAA).

They also propose to take control of the Department of Justice (DOJ), the Federal Bureau of Investigation (FBI), the Department of Commerce, the Federal Communications Commission (FCC) and the Federal Trade Commission (FTC), moving all of them under the Executive Branch reporting to the President.

The expansion of presidential power would undermine and destroy the existing balance of power built into our constitution that provides the guardrails against a dictatorial, authoritarian government.

Trump calls his political enemies vermin, pledging to *"root out the communists, Marxists, fascists, and the radical left thugs that live like vermin within the confines of our country,"* echoing dictators Hitler and Mussolini.

Robert Jones, founder of the Public Religion Research Institute warns *"What we have witnessed from Trump over the last few weeks is something new. Trump has clearly crossed into the domain of Nazi ideology openly."*

The following is the Project 2025 three-step process for gaining total power and setting the groundwork for the authoritarian takeover of the United States:

(1) Militarize the Justice Department by moving ALL Federal Law Enforcement Agencies to be directly accountable to the President

ANALYSIS: The objective is to fill the Justice Department with presidential appointees, loyalists unlikely to say "no" to controversial orders from the White House, and place new constraints on FBI authority transferring many of its responsibilities to other law enforcement agencies that are directly accountable to the President. The plan is to use the Justice Department to exact revenge on Trump's "enemies and political opponents, past and present."

The departments involved include Department of Justice (DOJ), Federal Bureau of Investigation (FBI), Department of Commerce, Federal Communications Commission FCC), and Federal Trade Commission (FTC).

(2) Eliminate or Privatize Independent Agencies

ANALYSIS: The objective is to eliminate agencies that would stand in the way of the expansion and deregulation of banks, big corporations, and especially the fossil fuel industry.

The departments involved include Consumer Financial Protection Bureau, the Transportation Security Administration (TSA), the Environmental

Protection Agency (EPA), the Department of the Interior (DOI), Housing and Urban Development (HUD), the Department of Education (DOE), and the National Oceanographic and Atmospheric Administration (NOAA).

This kind of reorganization—dismantling or eliminating Agencies and Departments—has been tried before by other presidents, during other administrations. Those who aspired to "restructure the government" soon learned that Departments and Agencies were easier to create than eliminate.

Over the last half-century, efforts to dismantle cabinet departments have been successful only once, when the Post Office Department was replaced with the United States Postal Service.

From the CRS Report for Congress-R42852:

> *"Between 1932 and 1981, Congress periodically delegated authority to the President that allowed him to develop plans for reorganization of portions of the federal government and to present those plans to Congress for consideration under special parliamentary procedures. Under these procedures, the President's plan would go into effect unless one or both houses of Congress passed a resolution rejecting the plan, a process referred to as a legislative veto."*

In 1984, the mechanism was amended to <u>require Congressional action</u> in order for a plan to go into *force.*

In 1995, the GOP took control of Congress, and promised to eliminate some of the same agencies targeted in the current Project 2025: Dept of Commerce, Dept of Education, Dept of Energy, and Housing and Urban Development.

They started with the Department of Commerce. The process involved eleven committees, and took months. Finally the bill had made it through all the committees and passed the house, but was stalled in the Senate when the chair of a critical committee, a Representative from Alaska, told of the unintended consequences it would mean for his state.

After all the time and energy invested, Congress lost interest and never went back to address the other agencies.

In 2012, then President Obama asked Congress for the power to consolidate parts of the federal government, calling for the merger of several trade and commerce-related agencies, a move estimated to eliminate more than 1,000 jobs and save $3 billion over 10 years. In the 2012 election, Democrats retained slight control in the Senate, but Republicans held control of the House. The proposal was killed.

The Clinton Administration's major reorganization effort in the 1990s, the NATIONAL PERFORMANCE REVIEW, pretty much "died on the vine" due to the difficulty in getting congressional support for such a major structural reorganization; plus the recognition that it would take so long to show results that it was not worth the effort. However, the Clinton administration was successful in eliminating several outdated agencies, such as the Interstate Commerce Commission, the Tea Tasters Board, and the Bureau of Mines.

Even Trump has tried this before. During his first administration he planned to eliminate dozens of government programs and defund 19 independent agencies. On 13 March 2017, he signed the PRESIDENTIAL EXECUTIVE ORDER ON A COMPREHENSIVE PLAN FOR REORGANIZING THE EXECUTIVE BRANCH, calling for the director of the Office of Management and Budget to consult with agency heads and within a year develop a plan for improving government efficiency that would "include recommendations to eliminate unnecessary agencies, components of agencies, and agency programs, and to merge functions." The plan was finalized in June 2018, but in the mid-term election of 2018 the Democrats took over Congress. The proposal died a natural death.

In summary, the President cannot dismantle, eliminate, or privatize Independent Agencies, or Departments without consent of Congress.

(3) Eliminate Federal Civil Service Employees and Replace Them with Political Loyalists

ANALYSIS: The objective is to reinstate a Trump Administration Executive Order known as "Schedule F," that would allow the President to strip non-partisan career civil servants of their civil service rights and protections and replace them with political loyalists who are "ideologically aligned with the President."

In April 2024 the Biden administration, in anticipation of another Trump administration, announced a final rule issued by the Office of Personnel Management (OPM), clarifying that nonpartisan career civil servants with protected status can't have that status taken away, and preventing nonpartisan career civil servants from being reclassified as political appointees. This rule prevents future Presidents from gutting the workforce and replacing career civil service workers with political appointees. It clarifies that policymaking classifications cannot be applied to nonpartisan career civil servants, only to non-career political appointees—the president only has the authority to fire individuals that he/she hires. The rule could theoretically STILL be overturned by a future president—though experts say that would likely result in a lengthy legal challenge lasting longer than a presidential term.

In any authoritarian society, the possessor of power dictates, and if you try and step outside, he will come after you.

~Salman Rushdie

THE DETAILS

The 992-page document has been broken down here into easy-to-find subject-matter categories. Each category includes the MAJOR proposed changes, including an analysis of the impact the change would make.

The following is NOT a comprehensive list of proposed changes, just those most critical to maintaining our democracy and freedoms.

"Recognizing that abortion is a sensitive issue and that people can hold good-faith views on all sides, we believe that government should be kept out of the matter, leaving the question to each person for their conscientious consideration."

~LIBERTARIAN PARTY PLATFORM

Abortion/ Contraception

A woman living in New England in the 17th - 18th centuries faced no legal, social or religious restriction on her decision about whether or not she would carry a child to term. The Puritan views on abortion came with them from England, where the procedure was legal until quickening—roughly 16-20 weeks.

Laws regarding abortion before quickening were not passed until the mid-1860s, triggered, by ethnic concerns among white Fundamentalist Christian Nationalists who (like today) became alarmed by the country's growing population of non-whites and declining birth rates among white, American-born, Protestant women. By 1880, all states had enacted laws restricting abortion, and by 1910, abortion was illegal at every stage of pregnancy in every state in the country.

In 1965, the U.S. Supreme Court overturned a law banning the distribution of birth control to married couples, ruling the law violated their right to privacy under the U.S. Constitution. It wasn't until 1972 that the Supreme Court overturned a law that prohibited the distribution of contraceptives to unmarried adults and single women finally had access to birth control.

On Jan 22, 1973, the U.S. Supreme Court struck down a Texas law banning abortion, the case known as Roe v. Wade—a landmark decision that effectively legalized abortion across the entire United States. The court held that a woman's right to an abortion was implicitly covered in the 14th Amendment's right to privacy clause.

On Jun 24, 2022, the U.S. Supreme Court overturned Roe v. Wade holding that women's privacy rights were no longer covered under the Constitution.

The Project 2025 proposed actions would not just institute a national abortion ban, but would turn back the clock to the late 1800s, prohibiting ALL types of contraception (male, female, married or single); ban stem cell medical research, IVF, tubal ligations, and vasectomies; and monitor all OB/GYN visits for possible violations.

(1) Reform the National Institutes of Health (NIH) "according to conservative principles."

> *ANALYSIS: The main focus here is on abortion and gender-affirming care. The "conservative principles," as defined by white Fundamentalist Christian Nationalists, are focused, not on what's best for the*

country or supporting individual rights and liberties, but on imposing their interpretation of right and wrong on the entire country.

(2) Pass a law prohibiting ALL stem cell research

ANALYSIS: There are two classifications of stem cell research: embryonic and non-embryonic. Amniotic, induced pluripotent, and adult stem cells do not involve the creation or destruction of a human embryo. Even embryonic stem cells can be collected without the destruction of an embryo using stem cells found in the umbilical cord, in breast milk, or even in bone marrow.

Stem cell research looks promising for finding cures for untreatable conditions ranging from Alzheimer's disease to Parkinson's disease, possibly even mental health issues, such as schizophrenia.

There is also the possibility of changing the embryonic development process, correcting chromosomal concerns, birth defects, and other errors in development before birth, while reducing the risks of pregnancy loss and health risks to the mother.

By prohibiting research in this area, we not only stand to lose the opportunity for significant advances in medical research, it will put us at a disadvantage internationally as other, more advanced research is done in places like China, forcing the United States to become dependent on other countries for cures, medicines and treatment.

(3) Ban ALL abortion services performed by the VA

ANALYSIS: The VA currently offers abortion counseling. Abortions are only available when the life or health of the mother would be endangered if the pregnancy were carried to term, or when the pregnancy is the result of rape or incest. Project 2025 would prohibit coverage in ALL cases.

(4) Ban ALL forms of contraceptives

ANALYSIS: Justice Thomas has argued that the Court should reconsider and overturn Griswold v Connecticut, a 1965 landmark decision that recognized the right of <u>married people</u> to obtain contraceptives. Even with the current constitutional protections of Griswold in place, it's uncertain what will happen with certain contraceptive methods, such as IUDs, birth control pills, and emergency contraceptive pills, even vasectomies and condoms, should the Republican Party take control.

(5) Direct FDA to revoke approval of abortion drug mifepristone and criminalize its use

ANALYSIS: Approved by the FDA in 2000, Mifepristone is used in more than half of the abortions in the United States. It has proven safer and less expensive than surgical abortions especially in the case of naturally occurring fetal mortality when the fetus is non-viable. The drug is sometimes prescribed to increase the likelihood that patients having a miscarriage won't need to undergo a more invasive procedure. It is also FDA-approved to treat Cushing's syndrome, and clinical trials currently underway indicate that it may be an effective treatment for breast cancer, brain cancer, prostate cancer, alcoholism, post-traumatic stress disorder and depression, among other conditions, all of which will be illegal if the drug itself is made illegal.

(6) Require states to monitor and report ALL abortions to the federal government for possible prosecution

ANALYSIS:This is a form of <u>government surveillance</u> and may run afoul of the Privacy Act of 1974 and the Constitution. The HIPAA Privacy Rule provides federal standards to safeguard the privacy of personal health information and gives patients an array of rights with respect to that information. However, the U.S. Department of Health & Human Services' Office of Civil Rights oversees compliance with HIPAA privacy requirements. If a nationwide abortion ban goes into effect, abortions will be illegal making it a reportable crime which will override the HIPAA rule. Natural (miscarriages) and induced abortions (for any reason) would also need to be reported creating a "chilling" effect for both doctors and patients.

We are already seeing obstetricians—including those who specialize in handling complex and risky pregnancies—leaving red states like Texas, Oklahoma and Tennessee where abortions have been banned or seriously restricted. They are reluctant to practice in states where they can be prosecuted for practicing medicine.

(7) Use the Comstock Act (an 1873 Victorian-Era bill) to prosecute those who send or receive contraceptives, abortion pills or equipment through the mail

ANALYSIS: Legal scholars have expressed concern that the restrictions go far beyond matters of the U.S. mail and Mifepristone by eliminating access to ALL forms of contraception—birth control and morning-after pills, hormonal implants, diaphragms, cervical caps and contraceptive sponges, spermicides, vaginal gels, condoms and even surgical tubal ligation and vasectomies (due to the restriction on "equipment"). It's possible that a court could interpret the Comstock Act to prevent the distribution of anything that could be used for birth control or abortion, anywhere in the U.S.—not just a de-facto abortion ban, but a nationwide contraception ban.

(8) Bar federal funds from being used to provide healthcare coverage for abortion or abortion-related medical procedures in ALL cases

ANALYSIS: Established in 1970, Title X was created

to provide affordable birth control and reproductive health care to low income women. Since 1977, no federal funding has been used for abortions.. The Hyde Amendment prohibits the use of federal funds for abortions except in the case of rape, incest or a threat to the pregnant person's life. However, since Medicaid is a federal-state partnership, some states do use state Medicaid funds to cover abortions that are deemed medically necessary. If a national abortion ban is passed, depending on the wording, women who are bleeding out due to miscarriage, have an ectopic pregnancy, have a non-viable fetus, or are carrying a dead fetus would be ineligible for care under Title X and/or Medicaid.

(9) Eliminate coverage of emergency contraception under the Affordable Care Act

ANALYSIS: This refers to the morning-after pill. These pills work mainly by delaying or preventing ovulation. They do NOT end a pregnancy that has already started.

(10) Replace the Biden administration's Reproductive Healthcare Access Task Force with a "pro-life task force"

ANALYSIS: Over the past decade, there has been an unprecedented number of laws enacted, regulations promulgated, and policies adopted that undermine access to sexual and reproductive health care services in the U.S. The Supreme Court's Dobbs decision has had a chilling impact on abortion access and other essential reproductive health services. In light of these challenges, the U.S. Department of Health and Human Services (HHS) has taken several meaningful actions under the Biden-Harris administration to protect and bolster sexual and reproductive health rights. The Reproductive Healthcare Access Task Force was formed to address these critical priorities.

The call to dismantle this task force and replace it with a pro-life task force signals the intent of Project 2025 to ban abortion at the national level.

(11) End the FACE Act

ANALYSIS: The Freedom of Access to Clinic Entrances Act (FACE) is a law signed by President Bill Clinton in May 1994 to address the violence, intimidation, and property damage to clinics and sanctuary churches by anti-abortion activists.

The Act prohibits: (1) the use of physical force, threat of physical force, or physical obstruction to intentionally injure, intimidate, interfere with or attempt to injure, intimidate or interfere with any person who is obtaining an abortion, (2) the use of physical force, threat of physical force, or physical obstruction to intentionally injure, intimidate, interfere with or attempt to injure, intimidate or interfere with any person who is exercising or trying to exercise their First Amendment right of religious freedom at a place of religious worship, (3) the intentional damage or destruction of a reproductive health care facility or a place of worship.

The desire by the Republican party to end this protection demonstrates anticipation, even plans, to re-activate the Fundamentalist Christian Pro-Life militants against pregnant women, healthcare providers, and religious leaders.

"Injustice anywhere is a threat to justice everywhere. We are caught in an inescapable network of mutuality, tied in a single garment of destiny. Whatever affects one directly, affects all indirectly."

~ Martin Luther King, Jr.
"Letter from Birmingham Jail"

Civil Rights

For months commentators and academics have been sounding the alarm on Project 2025 warning that it is *"a deeply racist endeavor that is aimed at dismantling many protections and aid programs for Americans of color."*

A close look at Project 2025, reveals that at least five of the named contributors have a history of anti-semitism, racist writings or statements, and/or white supremacist activity.

Writer and historian, Michael Harriot, warned, *"I read the entire Project 2025. Really, it's kind of a white supremacist manifesto."*

(1) Eliminate DEI (diversity, equity and inclusion) programs

ANALYSIS: The origins of DEI (Diversity, Equity, and Inclusion) can be traced back to the mid-1960s, a time of societal and legal changes in workplaces.

DEI programs promote the fair treatment and full

participation of all people, particularly groups who have historically been underrepresented or subject to discrimination on the basis of identity or disability.

Diversity includes gender, ethnicity, sexual orientation, disability, age, culture, or religion. Equity refers to fairness and justice, such as equal wages and benefits. Inclusion refers to an organizational culture where all employees feel heard, and have a sense of belonging and integration.

Banning of these types of policies in businesses and schools is the equivalent of condoning and encouraging discrimination, racism, misogyny, bullying, and sexual harassment.

(2) Rescind ALL civil rights protections on the basis of sexual orientation, gender identity, transgender status, and sex characteristics, and remove them from the "hate crime" classification

ANALYSIS: Eliminating laws and protections for the 13.9 million LGBTQ+ adults in the United States is unconscionable, opening them up to hate and violence. At a time when global acceptance of LGBTQ+ is on the rise, in America we are seeing a decline. That decline is largely driven by Fundamentalist Christian Nationalists in the Republican party who oppose the support of LGBTQ+ rights based on extremist, restrictive theological beliefs.

(3) Eliminate civil rights protections for people of color, mixed race, women, and non-Christians

ANALYSIS: The civil rights movement began in the late 1940s and resulted in one of the most significant legislative achievements in American history—the Civil Rights Act of 1964—a landmark civil rights and labor law that outlaws discrimination based on race, color, religion, sex, and national origin. It prohibits unequal application of voter registration requirements, racial segregation in schools and public accommodations, and employment discrimination. Project 2025 would work to overturn this law.

(4) Investigate and prosecute state and local governments, institutions of higher education, corporations, and private employers that provide protections or preferences under DEI programs

ANALYSIS: Looking at this another way, any organization that has a program favoring white, male, Christians would be safe, others would be subject to investigation by the DOJ.

This change would legalize and institutionalize (even MANDATE) discrimination against more than 90% of Americans in some manner. It would authorize Jim Crow laws, school segregation, pay inequality, and penalize individuals of non-Christian faith.

(5) Repeal HR 8404, The Respect for Marriage Act

ANALYSIS: HR 8404 is a landmark federal law passed in 2022 that codified the validity of same-sex and interracial marriages and provides a Federal definition of marriage as "between two individuals regardless of their sex, race, ethnicity, or national origin." It overturned the 1996 Defense of Marriage Act which defined marriage as strictly "between a man and a woman."

The Fundamentalist Christian Nationalists oppose same-sex marriage and same-sex parents adopting children based on their belief that marriage should be "a biblically based, social science-reinforced definition of marriage and family."

If HR 8404 was overturned and the Defense of Marriage Act reinstated, marriages between gay couples could be deemed illegal, all Federal protections and benefits removed, and children of those marriages could be classified as "illegitimate."

It could even result in adopted children of gay couples being removed from their adoptive parents.

(6) Prohibit federal funds from being used to provide gender-affirming care

ANALYSIS: In July 2023, Republicans in the U.S. House of Representatives passed two bills and released a third that denies gender-affirming care coverage for Medicare, Medicaid, TRICARE, the Indian Health Service (IHS), and the Department of Veterans Affairs

(VA). Together, these sources cover more than 40 percent of people in the U.S. The three bills ban virtually all federal sources from covering gender-affirming hormones and/or surgeries.

(7) The Department of Health and Human Services will be mandated to declare that "men and women are biological realities and married men and women are the ideal, natural family"

ANALYSIS: The "core values" as expressed in Project 2025 are wrapped in a 1950s vision of a nuclear family—a Caucasian Christian home composed of a working father, a homemaking mother, and their biological children—with no mixed race or same-sex pairings.

No individual or government entity has the authority to insert their personal religious beliefs into the formal description or mandate of a government office or agency. This is a clear violation of "separation of church and state" under the Constitution and would no doubt trigger multiple lawsuits.

This is especially true when the statement is entered with the intent to "deprive an individual, or group of individuals, of a legal right, privilege, or inherent franchise."

The climate is changing at a pace that's far faster than anything seen in 65 million years. If you think climate change isn't important, ask the Neanderthals. Oh, wait, all traces of Neanderthals disappeared about 40,000 years ago due to rapid climate change!

Climate/ Environment

We are the third largest country in the world by landmass—nearly as big as the entire continent of Europe; yet over half of the U.S. population lives in just nine states: California, Texas, Florida, New York, Pennsylvania, Illinois, Ohio, Georgia, and North Carolina.

Nearly one-third of all land in the United States—about 650 million acres—is federally owned. We have over 3.1 million square miles of forest land, and Lake Superior, on the United States-Canada border, is the largest body of freshwater in the world by surface area, covering 31,700 square miles. The United States is the only country that has all of Earth's five climate zones: tropical, dry, temperate, continental, and polar.

We have a responsibility to the rest of the world—to our planet—to care for and protect our large "chunk of land" on this big blue planet.

During the global pandemic we saw a significant decrease in greenhouse gas emissions that are now returning to pre-pandemic levels. According to the Global Carbon Budget report, the current rate of greenhouse gas pollution is so high that Earth has about 11 years to rein in emissions to avoid irreversible damage from climate change.

The following policies will result in environmental disasters such as we have never seen—floods, fires, hurricanes, tornadoes, mud slides, dried up river beds, soil erosion, etc. The overall impact of these dangerous and short-sighted policies will bring cataclysmic climate conditions.

Contrary to what former president Trump claims, over the past 10 years, we have become the world's largest petroleum producer, and the U.S. exports more petroleum than it imports.

The proposed Project 2025 policies are driven by the fossil fuel industry and the money they provide to the Republican party by eliminating requirements for meeting safe standards that protect our health and environment.

(1) Withdraw from the U.N. Framework Convention on Climate Change and the Paris Agreement

ANALYSIS: The Paris Agreement is an international treaty on climate change adopted in 2015. The treaty covers climate change mitigation, adaptation, and finance.

The United Nations Framework Convention on Climate Change (UNFCCC) signed in 1992 by 154 states at the United Nations Conference on Environment and Development. UNCED is an international treaty among countries for negotiating an agreement to limit dangerous climate change.

(2) Dismantle the National Oceanic and Atmospheric Administration (NOAA)

ANALYSIS: According to Project 2025, NOAA must be eliminated because "it is one of the main drivers of the climate change alarm industry, providing information and analysis about our changing environment and shining a light on the role of the fossil fuel industry"—major donors to the Republican Party.

The National Oceanic and Atmospheric Administration is a scientific and regulatory agency charged with forecasting weather, monitoring oceanic and atmospheric conditions, charting the seas, conducting deep-sea exploration, and managing fishing and protection of marine mammals and endangered species in the U.S. economic zone. This is the department responsible for issuing hurricane, tornado, severe storm and excessive heat warnings nationwide!

(3) Eliminate the Environmental Protection Agency (EPA)

ANALYSIS: The Mission of the EPA is to reduce environmental risks to ensure that Americans have clean air, land and water. It is responsible for administering and enforcing Federal laws protecting health and the environment; Providing access to information regarding human health and environmental risks; Ensuring that contaminated lands and toxic sites are properly cleaned up and revitalized; and reviewing chemicals in the marketplace for safety.

Project 2025's plan for eliminating programs, departments, offices and practices that ensure clean air, clean water, a safe and available food supply, is a recipe for disaster. We will see the return of deadly diseases like cholera, and dysentery from unsafe sources of water; high incidents of emphysema, COPD, asthma, bronchitis, and cancer from toxic chemicals in the air; illness and death from foodborne diseases and food poisoning.

While children, the elderly, and those with pre-existing conditions will be most at risk, no one is safe from the impact of chemicals in drinking water, polluted air, and poisoned food.

(4) Eliminate funding for climate research; Eliminate U.S. participation in "30 by 30" initiative

ANALYSIS: This is a worldwide initiative for governments to designate 30% of Earth's land and ocean area as protected areas by 2030 by expanding nature conservation efforts to mitigate climate change. More than 100 nations have agreed to the initiative.

Project 2025 is against this plan because it would stop clear-cutting of our forests, expansion of off-shore drilling, drilling on Native American lands, etc.

(5) Overturn "America the Beautiful" agenda and initiate fossil fuel development on lands owned by American Indians and Indian nations

ANALYSIS: The America the Beautiful Program is a plan for creating more parks and safe outdoor opportunities in nature-deprived communities. It supports Tribally led conservation and restoration priorities; Expands collaborative conservation of fish and wildlife habitats and corridors; Increases access for outdoor recreation; Incentivizes and rewards the voluntary conservation efforts of fishers, ranchers, farmers, and forest owners. It also creates jobs by investing in restoration and resilience projects and initiatives, including the Civilian Climate Corps.

(6) End sustainable food production development

ANALYSIS: Sustainable food production is "a method of production using processes and systems that are non-polluting, conserve non-renewable energy and natural resources, are economically efficient, are safe for workers, communities and consumers, and do not compromise the needs of future generations". The rationale behind Project 2025's objection is that "it promotes the climate change narrative and is supportive of climate change initiatives that cut into profits for the fossil fuel industry."

(7) Defund the Office of Energy Efficiency and Renewable Energy; Eliminate energy efficiency standards for appliances

ANALYSIS: The Office of Energy Efficiency and Renewable Energy is an office within the Department of Energy formed to drive the research, development, demonstration, and deployment of innovative technologies, systems, and practices that will help transition Americans to a 100% clean energy economy and ensure the clean energy economy benefits all Americans.

This Project 2025 mandate will result in every household paying more for gas and electricity to heat and cool the home, cook, or do laundry. However, fossil fuel industry profits will increase.

(8) Re-open energy and mineral production in the Thompson Divide of the White River National Forest, Colorado; the 10-mile buffer around Chaco Cultural Historic National Park in New Mexico; and the Boundary Waters area in northern Minnesota

ANALYSIS: This plan would violate a 2023 agreement between the Chaco Natives and the Biden Administration to withdraw public lands within a 10-mile radius of the park for 20 years, responding to decades of efforts from Tribes, elected officials, and the public to better protect the sacred and historic sites and Tribal communities currently living in northwest New Mexico. In 1987, Chaco Cultural Historic National Park, a social and religious center for the Chacoan peoples, was designated as a United Nations Educational, Scientific and Cultural Organization (UNESCO) World Heritage Site whose "outstanding natural and cultural resources form the common inheritance of all mankind."

(9) Eliminate SBA disaster relief loans to businesses damaged due to declared disasters (i.e. floods, hurricanes, tornados, etc.).

ANALYSIS: 99.9% of all businesses in the U.S. qualify as small businesses, collectively employing 47.3% of the nation's private workforce.

When a disaster hits, it affects everyone. Since most small businesses run on a tight budget, it can mean the end of the business. In the aftermath of a natural disaster it's been shown that small businesses are one of the hardest-hit sectors. Without the availability of an SBA loan, many of those businesses will close. When small businesses close en masse, the entire economy suffers. Like falling dominoes the result will be less tax income, a higher Federal deficit, a large spike in unemployment, and more home loan defaults.

(10) Eliminate long-term, low-interest SBA loans to homeowners and renters to rebuild or repair property due to damage from declared disasters (i.e. floods, hurricanes, tornados, etc.).

ANALYSIS: Currently homeowners are eligible for a disaster loan up to $200,000 for primary residence structural repairs or rebuilding. SBA may also be able to help homeowners and renters with up to $40,000 to replace important personal property, including automobiles damaged or destroyed in the disaster.

Even for homeowners with insurance coverage, it may not cover all the replacement, repair and rebuilding costs. A disaster loan could help cover the difference, including the policy deductible.

At a time when climate change is causing unprecedented natural disasters in all parts of the country, and insurance companies are either raising premiums, or refusing coverage altogether, this proposal would prove devastating to homeowners.

CRIME/SAFETY

Project 2025, makes multiple false claims, stating *"violent crime has increased across the United States,"* referring to *"catastrophic increases in crime,"* and *"the current crime wave."*

The reality is that crime has declined significantly over the past thirty years and is still going down. Both FBI and BJS data show dramatic declines since 1993: violent crime (-49%), property crime (-74%), aggravated assault (-39%) and murder (-34%).

The FBI data, comparing crime rates in the third quarter of 2023 to the same period last year, found that *"murder plummeted in the United States in 2023 at one of the fastest rates of decline ever recorded, and every category of major crime except auto theft declined. <u>The overall crime rate is at its lowest level since 1961."</u>*

(1) Eliminate the Department of Homeland Security (DHS)

ANALYSIS: While it's true that we depend on DHS to

address issues relating to immigration and border security, that's not the entire story. The Department of Homeland Security (DHS) tracks terrorism-related incidents, and shares intelligence on emerging terrorist threats with federal, state, and local governments and private entities.

Far-right domestic terrorism in the form of militant, nationalistic, white supremacist violent extremism continues to outpace all other types of terrorism and domestic violent extremism. As a result, much of the work of DHS in recent years has been focused on preparing for, preventing, and responding to domestic terrorism—defined by law as "involving criminal acts dangerous to human life on U.S. soil that appear intended to coerce a civilian population or influence or affect the conduct of government." The most obvious example is the January 6, 2021 attack on the Capitol.

Profiles of Individual Radicalization in the United States (PIRUS) data identified extremists associated with several anti-government movements, anti-Semitic movements, Second Amendment militias, the sovereign citizen movement, white supremacy, ecoterrorism, anarchism, the anti-abortion movement, the QAnon conspiracy theory movement, and the election denier movement.

The biggest threat as we head into the 2024 election is the election denier conspiracy movement that is a danger to our democracy at every level. It's well-

connected and well-funded. Groups like True the Vote and Michael Flynn's America Project are planning to mobilize thousands of Trump supporters if Trump loses in 2024, by again pushing baseless claims about election fraud. They are forming a terrorist militia similar to, but larger than, that of January 6 positioned throughout the country.

Efforts to eliminate the DHS are a dangerous threat to democracy and to the safety and security of every citizen.

(2) Dismantle the Transportation Security Administration (TSA)

ANALYSIS: The TSA was established in 2001 following the terrorist attacks on the World Trade Center. The TSA became part of the Department of Homeland Security (which is also scheduled for elimination) in March 2003, making up a quarter of the DHS workforce.

Along with screening more than 2 million passengers each day at nearly 440 airports nationwide, TSA safeguards all modes of land-based transportation: mass transit, freight rail, highway motor carrier and pipeline. Elimination of the agency will make us less safe when we travel, whether on our highways, railroads, mass transit, or in the air, and opens up more pathways for illegal smuggling operations.

(3) End the independence of the FBI and the

Department of Justice; Prohibit the FBI from investigating political "misinformation" or any political persons or party; "Gut" the FBI of individuals not sufficiently loyal to the president

ANALYSIS: Experts warn that amid an environment of rising authoritarianism, deep distrust, and political and social unrest the dangers from propaganda, falsehoods and conspiracy theories pose an unprecedented threat to democracy.

Project 2025 calls for a "top-to-bottom overhaul" of the Department of Justice and the FBI that gets rid of what it calls an "unaccountable bureaucratic managerial class and radical Left ideologues," proposing an agency that would be more focused on violent crime and filing litigation that's "consistent with the President's agenda" and filled with political appointees willing to do the President's bidding.

It also proposes prohibiting the FBI from investigating misinformation or making "politically motivated" moves against U.S. citizens (i.e., prosecuting individuals who are involved in insurrection activities such as the mob of January 6 or similar events).

(4) More active enforcement of the death penalty for more crimes

ANALYSIS: The death penalty still exists in many parts of the world. It's especially prevalent in countries with authoritarian rule.

When it comes to the death penalty, the United States is an outlier. While international law does not prohibit the death penalty, most democratic countries consider it a violation of human rights.

Some Justices of the Supreme Court have referred to international law as further affirmation of their own conclusions about the death penalty being a violation of "cruel and unusual punishment" under the Eighth Amendment.

More than 70% of nations globally have banned the practice altogether because it was deemed inhumane and archaic, and because it leaves no room for error. The National Academy of Sciences estimated that at least 4% of people sentenced to death are innocent.

The common rationale for the death penalty is that the threat of being executed in the future will cause potential offenders to refrain from committing a heinous crime. However, psychological and sociological research indicates that is not the case.

(5) Conduct an immediate, comprehensive review of all major active FBI investigations and activities and terminate any that are unlawful or contrary to the President's or national interest

ANALYSIS: This appears to be an effort aimed at shutting down and terminating investigations related to Donald Trump and others who participated in or were complicit in the January 6 insurrection, the efforts to overturn the 2020 election, the fake elector scheme and other offenses committed by members of the Trump administration and/or the Republican Party.

(6) Bring federal charges against criminals when local jurisdictions wrongfully allow them to evade responsibility for their conduct

ANALYSIS: Federal courts only have jurisdiction in one of two instances: when a federal question is presented or when the illegal act violated both state and federal laws, such as drug trafficking laws. Federal courts can also hear civil cases where various parties are from different states (interstate crimes). Otherwise this would be deemed illegal interference and a violation of the Constitutional right of an individual to a fair trial.

(7) Initiate Federal legal action against local officials—including District Attorneys—who refuse to prosecute criminal offenses in their jurisdictions

ANALYSIS: State and local law enforcement agencies are not subordinate to the FBI, and the FBI does not supervise or take over their investigations unless there is a Federal level "legal interest" in the crime. Efforts to impair or influence the prosecutorial discretion of a local District Attorney or any officer under his/her direction, would come under serious scrutiny from a Constitutional standpoint.

(8) Pursue legislation that encourages prosecution of violent crimes as well as appropriate sentences for such offenses

ANALYSIS: The decision to prosecute is made by a District Attorney based on the crime, the circumstances, and the evidence. Punishments for crimes are codified in the state penal code or statute. The length of a sentence is determined by a judge. If there is evidence that a particular judge is not following the statute, he/she can be impeached or recalled (depending on the state).

If a District Attorney is making bad decisions, this is a matter that falls to the governor, or is subject to impeachment or recall (depending on the state). The Federal government has no oversite role.

Federal legislation dictating state laws and sentencing guidelines/requirements would be a clear case of "federal overreach" and would come under scrutiny and no doubt end up before the Supreme Court.

(9) Secure the border which is the key entry point for many criminal organizations and their supplies, products, and employees

ANALYSIS: The claim that there are "many criminal organizations" coming across the border is just not true. The percentage of known criminals has changed little since 2015. Under the Trump administration roughly 2%, were found to have criminal backgrounds. Under the Biden administration to date just over 1% had criminal backgrounds. Under both administrations, the individuals were detained and sent back home.

Virtually no "supplies" or "products" have been found and seized from migrants seeking asylum. Research shows that most of the illicit drugs coming across the U.S.-Mexico border are smuggled through official ports of entry mostly by U.S. citizens, as well as other travelers who are legally authorized to cross.

Despite GOP political rhetoric, data related to migrant crime once they are in the U.S. doesn't point to a "migrant crime wave." Instead, criminologists have consistently found that immigrants commit crimes at a lower rate than native-born Americans.

(10) Restart the China Initiative

ANALYSIS: The China Initiative was launched under Attorney General Jeff Sessions in November 2018, with the goal of preventing industrial espionage from China. The DOJ promised aggressive pursuit of Chinese commercial theft.

Although there is no clear definition of what a "China Initiative" case is, most of the cases investigated involved researchers who failed to disclose Chinese funding on grant applications—many of them American professors at U.S. institutions. Some of the cases brought were based on false evidence provided by the FBI. In the three years of its operation (November 2018 through February 2022), no one was ever convicted or even charged with spying in any China Initiative case.

The Department of Justice announced the end of the program on February 23, 2022 due primarily to its lack of success in identifying any case of espionage or anything remotely resembling spying.

The Initiative has been criticized as racially profiling Chinese American citizens and other residents of Asian origin or ancestry, and placing them in danger.

"The message from history is so blatantly obvious—that free trade causes mutual prosperity while protectionism causes poverty—that it seems incredible that anybody ever thinks otherwise. There is not a single example of a country opening its borders to trade and ending up poorer."

~Matt Ridley

ECONOMY

Contrary to what the Republican party would have us believe, we are NOT "a nation in decline," or a "failed nation." The United States has the strongest economy in the world, and recovered from COVID quicker and with less impact than any other nation.

We are home to less than 5% of the world's population, yet the United States accounts for approximately 25% of global economic output.

- The Real gross domestic product (GDP) increased at an annual rate of 2.8 percent in the second quarter of 2024 (the ideal GDP growth rate is 2%-3%).
- The stock market continues to rise setting new records, signaling a likely September interest rate cut and a "soft landing" from the effects of the pandemic.

Although we are one of the most affluent nations on the planet and home to more billionaires than any other country—boasting seven of the world's 10 richest people—our general population is **not** among the richest in the world.

The term "trickle down" economics was popularized in the United States in reference to the economic policies of Ronald Reagan. The policies are based on the idea that spending by the wealthy and large corporations will "trickle down" to those less fortunate and generate stronger economic growth. Political scientists agree that the "trickle down" concept *"has been the most enduring **failed** policy idea in all of American politics...and in fact lowering taxes on the top 20% has been shown to actually **reduce** growth."*

Although Project 2025 is long on rhetoric and short on substance and detail, based on historical evidence, economists can pretty accurately predict the effects of these proposed changes on the economy.

The policies proposed by Project 2025 are just more of the same failing policies tried in the past and, just like in the past can be expected to trigger another economic downturn possibly equaling that of the Great Recession or even the Depression of the 1930s.

(1) Reform the Federal Reserve turning power back to the banks and returning to the gold standard

ANALYSIS: This proposal advocates economic decisions that duplicate those that in the past resulted in economic disaster for the country.

The Great Recession of 2007-2009, the worst global

economic crisis since the Great Depression resulted from a combination of tax cuts, spending increases, and corporate greed in the banking industry due to lack of governmental oversite.

The Great Depression of the 1930s, the worst economic downturn in U.S. history, was caused by several factors, including the gold standard, and the 1929 Smoot-Hawley Act that raised U.S. tariffs by an average of 16 percent—<u>a disastrous economic policy that Trump has promised to repeat if he is re-elected!</u>

The U.S. came off the gold standard for domestic transactions in 1933 and ended international convertibility of the dollar to gold in 1971 when President Richard Nixon announced that the United States would no longer convert dollars to gold at a fixed value, thus completely abandoning the gold standard.

(2) Eliminate the Consumer Financial Protection Bureau (CFPB)

ANALYSIS: The Consumer Financial Protection Bureau (CFPB) is an independent bureau within the Federal Reserve, authorized by the Dodd-Frank Wall Street Reform and Consumer Protection Act in 2010 as a legislative response to the financial crisis of 2007-08 and the subsequent Great Recession. It is responsible for consumer protection in the financial sector, including banks, credit unions, securities firms, payday lenders, mortgage-servicing operations, foreclosure relief services, debt collectors, for-profit colleges, and other financial companies operating in the United States.

The CFPB writes and enforces rules for financial institutions, examines both bank and non-bank financial institutions, monitors and reports on markets, as well as collects and tracks consumer complaints.

Eliminating the CFPB would undermine much of what the Bureau has done to protect consumers since its beginning—protecting consumers from junk fees, risky mortgages, discriminatory practices, predatory lenders, abusive debt collectors, etc. Consumers would be left to the mercy of the "money lenders."

EDUCATION/ CHILDCARE

Various federal laws and the courts and lawmakers interpretation of the 10th Amendment, prohibits the federal government from directly regulating school curricula, educational standards or establishing schools or colleges. School districts operate under rules established by state governments, so it's unclear exactly how some of the following objectives could be legally implemented.

(1) Eliminate the Department of Education, including Title I which supplements state and local education funding for low-income students

ANALYSIS: The over-arching objective of this proposed action is to advance the concept of private school choice (especially religious schools) paid for through increases in local and Federal taxes.

Eliminating this department changes the entire

fabric of federal education policymaking and how federal education laws are enforced. It would take away federal standards and allow states to opt out of any or all federal education programs and devote their share of federal education funds to other purposes.

It would scale back the federal government's ability to enforce civil rights laws like Title IX, which prohibits sex-based discrimination, discrimination on the basis of sexual orientation/gender identity, and Title VI, which prohibits race-based discrimination, effectively opening the way for a return to school segregation.

Eliminating this Department will also remove funding for children with disabilities (IDEA), early childhood education (Head Start), Pell Grants, No Child Left Behind, work assistance, and other programs serving special needs children and children in poverty.

(2) Establish a national "school choice" policy that directs public funds to be used for students to attend private or religious schools

ANALYSIS: Using public funds to subsidize religious schools violates the separation of church and state. A survey of parents who currently use school vouchers showed that the number one reason parents chose to use vouchers was "religious environment and instruction."

It's been shown that voucher programs can cost the state millions of dollars and result in increased local income tax and property taxes. Studies have also shown that a growing number of voucher students are not low-income, but from suburban, middle class families who already have access to good public schools, or already have their children in a private school.

Unlike public schools, private schools do not have to accept children with special needs, and if they do, many require extra fees (billed to the parents). Private schools are not required by law to accommodate students who need extra or enhanced instruction, special services or equipment, or other educational accommodations such as following the Americans with Disabilities Act (ADA), Individuals with Disabilities Education Act (IDEA), and Individualized Education Plans (IEPs).

In addition to the threat of underfunding of public schools, the "school choice" concept is firmly grounded in racism and would result in de facto school segregation. Schools receiving vouchers are allowed to "pick and choose" what children they accept, creating educational wastelands of highly segregated school districts along racial, ethnic and socioeconomic lines.

(3) Prohibit the use of Federal dollars to fund critical race theory training (CRT)

ANALYSIS: This is a nonsensical, ludicrous proposal for a law against something that doesn't even exist:

(a) CRT is a **legal analysis and research class** *taught in law schools*
(b) CRT is NOT now, nor has it ever been, taught in any elementary, middle or high school
(c) No federal dollars have ever been used to fund CRT "training." since there is no such thing

Christopher Ferguson Rufo, a writer-contributor to Project 2025, is the right-wing extremist, self-described "fascist thinker" frequently seen on Fox News who started the "CRT conspiracy" madness.

His admitted goal was to, in his words, "put all of the various cultural insanities under that brand category in order to have the public read something crazy in the newspaper and immediately think critical race theory, in order to generate public school distrust and racist fears."

Through the spread of false claims about CRT, he could promote the concept of "school choice" (your tax dollars can be used to fund my child's attendance at a private school, charter school, or religious school).

The underlying intent of the anti-CRT movement to justify "school choice" is to get around the Brown vs Board of Education, Civil Rights Act of 1964 which bans school segregation.

CRT is a "CODE WORD" used to hide the racist intent behind the banning of racial history, social integration, and racial equality, and to justify discriminatory policies in schools and businesses. It has been distorted and misapplied to include any reference to race or racial history, labeling everything from the history of slavery, the Civil War, the Mexican-American War, American Indian Wars, the civil rights movement and laws, as CRT, and claiming it's an "anti-white conspiracy by the forces of wokeness trying to brainwash school children."

Anti-CRT efforts have resulted in acts of violence against teachers, school boards, and librarians, and contributed to the simultaneous book banning mania.

(4) Eliminate the Head Start Program

ANALYSIS: The Head Start Program offers free early childhood education, health and nutrition services to children from low-income families, indigenous Americans on reservations, and homeless children. It is the oldest and largest program of its kind helping to create healthy development and early childhood education in low-income children ages three to five.

The program includes health screenings, check-ups, eye examinations and dental check-ups. Studies show that participants in Head Start have substantially improved test scores, substantially higher high school and college completion and higher incomes as adults than similar children who did not attend.

Eliminating this program would negatively impact the families of 800,000+ children, two-thirds of whom are Black, Hispanic, Latino, or indigenous American. It would undermine local and national economic growth and exacerbate inequalities among families with young children, especially in rural communities with "child care deserts."

It's estimated that without Head Start, these families would have to spend almost $12,000 more a year resulting in many single parent families withdrawing from the workplace and going on welfare.

It would have an especially devastating effect on some of the most vulnerable children in the country—children in foster care, homeless children, and children with disabilities, who fill at least 10 percent of enrollment slots in Head Start programs.

(5) Cut Federal funding for free and reduced school meal programs

ANALYSIS: The Project seeks to limit the number of children who can qualify for free school meal programs and proposes condensing all of the programs into a single block grant for each individual state, claiming a block grant approach would give states flexibility to allocate the funds as they see fit. Since a block grant approach would require an annual appropriation by Congress, states would be less able to address variables like more lower-income students moving into a school district, or rising food costs.

Last year, the entire federal free school lunch program cost an estimated $28.7 billion—far beyond the total annual state block grant payment being proposed. Individual states would be expected to make up the shortfall resulting in increased state and/or property taxes.

(6) Eliminate subsidies for family child care (FCC)

ANALYSIS: Family Child Care (FCC) is child care offered in a provider's home. FCC is currently serving more than 10 million children nationwide. According to the Office of Childcare, losing the FCC option would significantly impact low-income families with parents who work nontraditional hours, live in rural communities, have infants and toddlers, or who do not speak English as their primary language.

Working mothers make up a significant part of the labor force, accounting for nearly one-third (32%) of all employed women mostly in the educational, health care and social service sectors. In 2021, there were 24.2 million mothers in the U.S. labor force with children younger than 18. Having even a percentage of these women leave the workforce would create a massive labor shortage negatively impacting the economy.

The effect on FCC providers would be devastating. Between 2005 and 2017 more than 97,000 licensed family child care homes closed. For many FCC providers, this is their sole source of income. A change such as suggested would result in more closures exacerbating an already existing daycare crisis.

(7) Enact legislation allowing parents to sue schools based on what they are teaching

ANALYSIS: Anyone can sue for anything in America. The question in this case is whether the parents or the school board is the decision-maker regarding the educational curriculum and whether or not a particular subject is in compliance with the mandated curriculum.

Whether K-12 educators and state and local school boards have any legally protected right to set a curriculum with standards of how and what to teach is sure to be tested soon.

(8) Eliminate the Public Service Student Loan Forgiveness Program, the income driven repayment program; and the Biden-Harris SAVE initiative

ANALYSIS: The United States has the world's strongest higher education system of any country drawing more than a million international students a year. For decades, the U.S. government has helped students finance their higher education to bolster the country's economic competitiveness and national security.

In March of 2020, President Trump suspended interest accrual for government-held federal student loans, and along with the CARES Act and two more executive orders extended the interest freeze to January 31, 2021. When Biden took office, he extended the interest moratorium to September 30, 2021.

U.S. student loan debt has ballooned in recent years, outpacing most other forms of consumer borrowing, leading to concerns about the impact they have on the American economy.

Roughly one in five Americans hold student debt ranging from about $30,000 to more than $100,000. Many borrowers have been paying on loans for years and due to fees and interest still owe more than the original amount of the loan.

History shows that student loan debt slows consumer spending of all kinds, especially with regard to large purchases like buying a home or a car. The absence of these expenditures limits the economic growth of businesses that would have profited from them and the GDP growth of the nation.

Student loan debt has also been shown to result in delays in starting a family. The Heritage Foundation's focus on "family values" seems short sighted when they object to actions that would lead to higher household incomes and better, more stable, families.

EMPLOYMENT/WAGES

Project 2025 is anti-Union and anti-worker, and the proposed policies are contrary to good economic practices. Notably missing is any reference to the minimum wage, an issue that affects all working families. The only reference is a generic statement *"encouraging wages and conditions for jobs that can support a family."*

Instead Project 2025 blames low wages on *"the constant flow of illegal immigration [that] suppresses the wages"*—a concept that has been disproven time and again.

(1) End project labor agreements; and repeal Davis-Bacon wage requirements

> *ANALYSIS: This proposal is an attempt to undermine the Biden administration's Bipartisan Infrastructure Law of 2021, which is funding many federal infrastructure projects.*
>
> *The Davis-Bacon and Related Acts (DBRA) require*

payment of local prevailing wages to construction workers performing work on federally funded construction projects. On Aug 8, 2023 the U.S. Department of Labor (DOL) issued a final rule to raise the prevailing wage standard for approximately 1 million construction workers.

(2) Reintroduce the Teamwork for Employees and Managers (TEAM) Act of 2022

ANALYSIS: The Republican authored Teamwork for Employees and Managers Act would provide employers with a new union-avoidance tool—and another way for employers to get around the National Labor Relations Act.

The "TEAM" Act would amend labor law to legalize employee involvement organizations as an "alternative to employee unionization." The employee organization would be incapable of engaging in collective bargaining, and could be dissolved at any time at the employer's sole discretion. Historically, employers have found this an effective strategy for preempting the organization of independent labor unions.

Two-thirds of U.S. workers are either eager to unionize, or open to doing so. The fact that roughly a third of unorganized American workers would like to be in a union suggests that adverse organizing conditions are keeping organized labor down. The TEAM Act is just another attempt at preventing unionization and offers nothing that improves wages, conditions or benefits for employees.

(3) Allow employers to calculate overtime over a longer period

ANALYSIS: Employers would not be required to pay overtime for extra hours worked, but could allow employees to take compensatory time instead.

This is an effort to bypass the Federal Fair Labor Standards Act (FLSA). When an employee works overtime he/she is to be paid time and a half or double time. Taking compensatory time ignores the "time and a half" or "overtime" requirement and just compensates with an "equal" amount of time off.

(4) Set a cap of $12,000 per year <u>or lower</u> on employer-paid benefits (including benefits for dependents aged 23 or over) that employers can claim as deductions

ANALYSIS: The claim is that this would incentivize employers to raise salaries. The reality is this will just push the burden onto the worker while the employer pockets the savings. As for the health insurance coverage for dependents aged 23 or older, this proposal would put a tremendous burden on families with children or family members who have special needs, are still in college, or who are working at minimum-wage jobs that don't provide health insurance benefits.

(5) Transform the H-1B program to bring in the "best and brightest" from other countries at the highest wages.

ANALYSIS: This program would pay workers from other countries higher wages than American workers, increasing competition for those same jobs.

(6) Rescind ALL DEI regulations prohibiting discrimination in hiring, firing, promotions, or wages

ANALYSIS: (See "Civil Rights" Chapter)

(7) Cap and phase down the H-2A visa program

ANALYSIS: The Project 2025 proposed action would lead to significant farm failures, food shortages, and higher consumer prices. It would also lead to higher farm subsidies, increasing the Federal deficit.

The United States lost 141,733 farms over the last five years, in part due to worker shortage. The H-2A visa program that allows non-immigrant foreign workers into the U.S. for temporary agricultural jobs, continually falls short, especially for farmers in year-round operations like dairy and livestock.

This plan would exacerbate an existing crisis and lead to more farm failures in regional agricultural states.

Housing/ Homelessness

Housing costs and homelessness are among the top concerns for Americans, but curiously are not specifically addressed in Project 2025, other than plans to *"dismantle the Federal Housing Administration (FHA) and initiate a HUD task force consisting of politically appointed personnel to identify and reverse all actions taken by the Biden Administration that addresses housing and homelessness."*

In January 2023 the Department of Housing and Urban Development (HUD) reported 653,104 homeless Americans in its annual point-in-time report. Apparently the "great minds" of the Heritage Foundation have no suggestions about what to do about, or how to address, the reality that about one in every 500 Americans is experiencing homelessness, including Veterans who experienced homelessness at a slightly higher rate than the overall population. Twenty-two out of every 10,000 veterans are homeless, despite the VA housing program for homeless Vets.

(1) Dismantle the Department of Housing and Urban Development (HUD)

ANALYSIS: The Department of Housing and Urban Development, was established September 9, 1965. The Agency is responsible for a wide-range of housing-related services, including (but not limited to) Community Development Block Grants (CDBG); the HOME program, Shelter Plus Car; Emergency Shelter Grants (ESG); Section 8 Housing; the Federal Housing Administration (FHA); Supportive Housing for the Elderly (Section 202); Supportive Housing for Persons with Disabilities (Section 811); Indian Housing: Office of Fair Housing and Equal Opportunity; Government National Mortgage Association (Ginnie Mae); Healthy Homes and Lead Hazard Control.

This office also enforces federal laws against discrimination in housing based on race, color, religion, national origin, sex, disability, and familial status.

Eliminating HUD will impact MILLIONS of individuals and exacerbate the housing crisis, leading to increased homelessness, especially in large cities where home costs and rentals are already a problem.

(2) Immediately end the Biden Administration's Property Appraisal and Valuation Equity (PAVE)

task force

ANALYSIS: PAVE is a Task Force focused on identifying concrete actions that agencies can take to eliminate bias and advance equity in home appraisals that have contributed to a gap between the values of homes in communities of color and predominantly white neighborhoods.

(3) Repeal the Affirmatively Furthering Fair Housing (AFFH) regulation

ANALYSIS: Title VIII of the Civil Rights Act of 1968, known as the Fair Housing Act, requires HUD and recipients of federal funds from HUD to affirmatively further the policies and purposes of the Fair Housing Act.

The regulation directs HUD to ensure that the agency and its program participants proactively take meaningful actions to overcome patterns of segregation, promote fair housing choice, eliminate disparities in opportunities, and foster inclusive communities free from discrimination.

Repealing this regulation would open up opportunities for large corporations and investors who hold property and receive HUD funds to raise rents and freely discriminate on the basis of color, gender, sexual orientation, etc.—repeating the long-standing pattern of housing discrimination.

(4) Eliminate the new Housing Supply Fund

ANALYSIS: In May of 2022 the Biden Administration released a Housing Supply Action Plan to build more housing, lower costs, and provide financing for affordable housing production to develop 500,000 units of housing for low- and moderate-income renters and homebuyers.

The key concepts of the Housing Supply Action Plan are to: Reward jurisdictions that have reformed zoning and land-use policies; Deploy new financing mechanisms to build and preserve more housing where financing gaps currently exist; Expand and improve existing forms of federal financing; Ensure that more government-owned supply of homes and other housing goes to owners who will live in them.

Under the Housing Supply Action Plan more units are under construction than at any time in over 50 years, and the rate of new housing starts is up 17 percent compared to the last Administration.

Discontinuing this program is disingenuous and contrary to common sense. The only basis for shutting it down is political.

(5) Prohibit noncitizens, including all mixed-status families, from living in federally assisted housing

ANALYSIS: It is already the law that non-citizens who

do not hold a Green Card (authorization to live and work in the United States) are not eligible for public housing assistance of any kind.

(6) Restrict first-time homebuyer eligibility for single family housing programs across federal agencies and government-sponsored enterprises

ANALYSIS: In a situation where homelessness is a problem, and many families are unable to buy a home, this proposal seems counter-intuitive.

I had always hoped that this land might become a safe and agreeable asylum to the virtuous and persecuted part of mankind, to whatever nation they might belong.

~George Washington

IMMIGRATION

We have one of the most diverse populations of any country in the world, and are home to nearly 45 million immigrants. We are a country of immigrants and have been since the beginning.

Although approximately 43 million Americans identify as ancestrally German, that demographic is changing. New Census Bureau projections predict that the U.S. will be minority white by 2045. These are the statistics that frighten the white Fundamentalist Christian Nationalists.

Trump adds fuel to the fear with the words Hitler used about the Jews, claiming immigration is *"poisoning the blood of our country."* Claiming *"people are coming in with disease."* and *"they're destroying our country."*

On February 4, 2024 Congress passed a bi-partisan border security bill with the most significant changes in U.S. immigration and border security in decades. Mitch McConnell, the top Senate Republican, supported the negotiations, saying *"Republicans would not get a better deal under a Republican White House."*

Unfortunately, Republicans in Congress sank their own border control bill, in order to please Donald Trump. James Lankford (R-OK), one of the primary authors of the bill, told Brett Baier on Fox News, *"It was painful to watch. President Trump said 'don't fix anything during the election, it's the single biggest issue during the election, don't resolve this.' "*

(1) Appropriate funding for border wall and system infrastructure in accordance with the Border Security Improvement Plan (BSIP)

> *ANALYSIS: In 2018 Congress required the Department of Homeland Security (DHS) to submit the BSIP for improving border security, including how the DHS intended to use personnel, barriers, and technology. DHS was required to include 11 elements in the plan, such as goals and objectives for security investments and a detailed implementation schedule.*
>
> *The Plan was late and 10 of the 11 elements were incomplete. It wasn't until well into the Biden administration that the required elements were provided by the DHS. In April 2022, Customs and Border Protection (CBP) provided Congress with a corrective action plan that addressed the missing elements. Funding for the BSIP was part of the bi-partisan bill presented on February 4, 2024 that was "tanked" by former president Trump.*

(2) Combine ALL immigration-related Agencies into a stand-alone Border and Immigration Agency that reports to the President

ANALYSIS: Regardless of whether the combining of similar agencies is a good idea or not, giving the President unfettered authority over the lives of men, women and children seeking asylum at the border is ripe for abuse especially when Trump is falsely claiming they are "bringing disease," "mentally ill," and is advocating "lethal force" and "migrant camps" as options.

(3) Give ICE Deportation officers authority to arrest, detain, and remove suspected immigration violators anywhere in the United States "without a warrant "

ANALYSIS: Rights under the Constitution apply equally to citizens and non-citizens. The rights of non-citizens under the Fourth and Fifth Amendments including due process and the right to a jury have been established. Arrest and detention without a warrant is a violation of the Constitution.

(4) Rescind ICE regulations prohibiting apprehension of migrants in schools, playgrounds, hospitals, churches or other sensitive locations.

ANALYSIS: This is a "slippery slope" and could open the door to abuse of power. Adult migrants can be arrested in all of these places <u>with a proper warrant</u>.

However, this policy could result in children being taken from school, a playground, etc. without the parents' consent. Under state and federal law, removing a child from their custodial parent or legal guardian is illegal—even if the parent is in the country illegally—it's kidnapping. Kidnapping is a Federal offense whether it's perpetrated by a police officer, an ICE agent or a stranger on the street.

As for apprehending migrant adults in any of these places, the police must first have a valid arrest warrant issued based on probable cause. They must reasonably believe that the suspect is on the premises, and they must follow specific regulations for that jurisdiction regarding other limitations to police entry into schools and churches.

(5) Use active-duty military personnel and the National Guard to help with arrest operations on the border.

ANALYSIS: Except for express constitutional authorization or Act of Congress the US military can't serve as another police force arresting migrants on site. The Posse Comitatus Act (PCA) specifically ***prohibits*** *the use of the armed forces to execute law on U.S. soil. The only exception is the U.S. Coast Guard which has law enforcement functions.*

The State police and National Guard—from any state, under any orders—have ***zero jurisdiction*** *to enforce federal immigration policy.*

(6) Eliminate T and U visas

ANALYSIS: Congress created "T" and "U" visas for victims of human trafficking and other crimes who have suffered mental or physical abuse and are willing to assist law enforcement and government officials in the investigation or prosecution of the criminal activity. Eliminating these incentives would result in a significant decrease in apprehension and conviction of human traffickers, drug smugglers, and other criminals.

(7) Move detention of alien children from Health and Human Services to Department of Homeland Security (DHS)

ANALYSIS: The DHS is scheduled per Project 2025 to be eliminated, so this plan makes no sense! During the Trump administration U.S. Customs and Border Protection carried out nearly half a million child detentions. More than 5,000 migrant children were separated from their families with no tracking process or records that would allow them to be reunited. Six years later, 1,400 children remain separated from their families.

This is a human rights violation that should never be allowed to happen again.

(8) Cap and phase down the H-2A visa program

ANALYSIS: (See Employment/Wages Chapter)

"If there is a poor man with you, one of your brothers, in any of your towns in your land which the Lord your God is giving you, you shall not harden your heart, nor close your hand from your poor brother;

~Deuteronomy 15:7

MEDICAID

Medicaid is a government program that provides health insurance for adults and children with limited income and resources.

Although the federal government sets baseline standards for state Medicaid programs, the program is partially funded and primarily managed by state governments.

Medicaid provides free health insurance to more than 85 million low-income and disabled people as of 2022. It also covers long-term services and support, including nursing home care and home- and community-based services. Qualifying disabilities may be cognitive, developmental, intellectual, mental, physical, sensory, or a combination of multiple factors. Disabilities can be present from birth or can be acquired during a person's lifetime.

Research shows that existence of the Medicaid program improves health outcomes and provides economic benefits to states and health providers.

(1) Cut funding and set a lifetime cap on Medicaid coverage

ANALYSIS: The plan calls for caps on how much federal funding states may receive to help pay for Medicaid costs, though it doesn't specify how such caps would be determined.

This would impact health care facilities and providers serving Medicaid patients including nurses, home care providers, emergency medical personnel and physicians as well as millions of beneficiaries.

It calls for setting time limits on Medicaid coverage and imposing lifetime caps on benefits "to disincentivise permanent dependence." This limit would severely affect individuals who are permanently disabled or who were born with severe disabilities.

The cap would ultimately result in federal Medicaid spending that does not keep pace with expected enrollment and health care cost increases, resulting in a significant cut to funding over time.

(2) Impose work requirements to receive coverage

ANALYSIS: Work requirements would add substantial bureaucratic red tape to Medicaid, putting coverage and health at risk for 21 million working-age Medicaid beneficiaries.

According to an HHS report, the vast majority of

working-age Medicaid enrollees are already employed, have a disability, are parents with childcare or caretaking responsibilities, or are in school.

The recommendation echoes a reform the Trump administration had pursued during his first term before being sued by a coalition of states and D.C.

Should any political party attempt to abolish social security unemployment insurance and eliminate labor laws and farm programs you would not hear of that party again in our political history. There is a tiny splinter group of course that believes you can do these things. Among them are a few other Texas oil millionaires and an occasional politician or business man from other areas. Their number is negligible and they are stupid.

~Dwight D. Eisenhower

MEDICARE/SOCIAL SECURITY

It's notable that Project 2025 fails to propose any solutions for Social Security claiming that its proposals for the program *"could not be covered here in depth."* Most likely it's not covered because of all the blowback they would get from seniors already receiving social security and individuals nearing retirement age.

To be clear, the authors/contributors to Project 2025 and the Heritage Foundation fervently support the idea of privatizing Social Security and raising the full retirement age to sixty-nine. Co-author, Stephen Moore, has advocated to *"slash and privatize"* Social Security. Kevin Roberts, the president of the Heritage Foundation, has admitted that Project 2025 is just the basis of their plan and *"there are parts of the plan that we will not share with the left."*

In March of 2024, the House Republican Study Committee (RSC) released its fiscal year 2025 budget proposal, which includes significant cuts to Social Security. Despite dedicating six pages on Social Security, the RSC document's policy proposals for the Social Security program were given just one sentence in one paragraph, *"for instance, the RSC Budget would also make modest adjustments to the retirement age for future retirees."*

The full retirement age (FRA) is currently 67, but plans put forward by the Republican Study Committee and the Heritage Foundation would raise the full retirement age to 69, with the median-wage retiree receiving thousands of dollars less per year.

(1) Make Medicare Advantage Plans (MAP) the default enrollment option

ANALYSIS: The Project 2025 objective is to privatize Medicare in order to shift the administration and price setting to private, profit-oriented insurance companies.

Medicare Advantage plans are a type of private insurance that boast low premiums and lots of other benefits you may or may not want or need—but that's not the whole story.

Even though Medicare Advantage plans cap out-of-pocket spending, there are high co-pays and deductibles. They have a smaller network of providers and lack of coverage outside of their service area. If you love your current doctor, there's a high probability he/she will not be part of the MAP.

They also have referral requirements if you need a specialist, making it more difficult to get the necessary care you may need.

It appears this change would eliminate the option for "gap insurance," since the basic Medicare on which gap insurance is based may no longer be available. Individuals currently on basic Medicare plus gap insurance should expect to see a HUGE increase in out-of-pocket costs.

(2) Restructure 340B drug subsidies toward beneficiaries rather than hospitals

ANALYSIS: The 340B Drug Pricing Program is a U.S. federal government program created in 1992 that requires drug manufacturers to provide outpatient drugs to eligible health care organizations and covered entities at significantly reduced prices.

For more than 30 years, the 340B Drug Pricing Program has provided financial help to hospitals serving vulnerable communities to manage rising prescription drug costs. This would especially impact small rural community hospitals, likely causing many of them to close.

(3) End the federal government's ability to negotiate drug prices; Repeal the $35 per month cap on insulin costs for seniors on Medicare; End

Medicare's $2,000 per year cap on out-of-pocket drug costs

ANALYSIS: The high out-of-pocket cost of drugs cause many Americans, particularly those with chronic conditions such as diabetes, to delay or skip taking needed treatments. Negotiating drug prices to match what other countries pay and passing it along to seniors is a no-brainer.

You would think this is a good thing, but for the GOP it's not. Big Pharma contributes millions to the GOP coffers and have a lot of influence over bills that are passed.

(4) Base Medicare payments on the health status of the patient or intensity of the service rather than where the patient happens to receive that service

ANALYSIS: The sicker you are, if you have a pre-existing condition, or your illness requires more frequent visits to the doctor, the higher your cost. This is how insurance companies work. It should NOT be how Medicare works.

(5) Repeal the Medicare Shared Savings Program

ANALYSIS: For older adults on a low or fixed income, this extra safety net can ease the financial stress associated with health care expenses. It ensures they can access the care they need without worrying about excessive costs.

Accountable Care Organizations (ACOs)—groups of physicians, hospitals, and others involved in patient care—are held accountable for the quality, cost, and experience of care of an assigned Medicare fee-for-service. The focus is on delivering the right care at the right time, while avoiding unnecessary services and medical errors. The successful ACO is eligible to share in the savings it achieves for the Medicare program.

Our liberty depends on the freedom of the press, and that cannot be limited without being lost.

~Thomas Jefferson

PUBLIC MEDIA

Freedom of speech as stated in the 1st and 14th Amendments to the Constitution of the United States, includes the right to express information, ideas, and opinions free of government restrictions based on content. Censorship of all kinds in the U.S. is at the highest rate seen in more than twenty years, and attacks on First Amendment freedoms are increasing across the country.

(1) Reform Section 230 which shields tech companies and social media networks from being sued over content on their platforms

ANALYSIS: Section 230 of Title 47 of the Federal Communications Commission generally provides immunity for online computer services with respect to third-party content generated by its users. At its core, Section 230(c)(1) provides immunity from liability for providers and users of an "interactive computer service" who publish information provided by third-party users stating "No provider or user of an interactive computer service shall be treated as the publisher or speaker of any information provided by another information content provider."

What is being proposed is currently under review and litigation with regard to violations of First Amendment rights.

(2) Defund the Corporation for Public Broadcasting (CPB)

ANALYSIS: One of the first signs of an authoritarian movement is taking control of public broadcasting in order to control the information available to the public.

Noncommercial radio and television stations in many localities struggle to survive. Defunding CPB would severely diminish, and likely destroy, public broadcasting service in the United States.

Its $500 million annual appropriation from the government helps support more than 1,500 locally controlled and operated public television and radio stations that ensure Americans have universal access to free non-commercial, unbiased, and uncensored, local public media.

(3) Shut down telecommunications companies that distribute "adult entertainment/pornography" and imprison the people who produce or distribute it

ANALYSIS: The Project 2025 objective is to reinstate 1950's censorship standards—a time when television series, variety shows, cartoons, and even commercials could be censored or banned for content that showed, made reference to, or suggestions of, sensuality, sexuality, bodily functions, recreational drug use, shared beds (even by married couples), an actress's navel, pregnancy (the word or condition), toilets, song lyrics, and even some cartoon characters.

Under a Fundamentalist Christian Nationalist administration, many of the popular sit-coms, series, and made-for-TV movies could be banned on the same basis as the recent book bans because of uncomfortable interpretations of history or reality (like the holocaust or slavery); stories that lead to political questioning (like A Gentleman In Moscow, or The Handmaid's Tale, or Fahrenheit 451); or stories about sexual abuse; or about questioning spirituality (like A Wrinkle in Time).

The Christian Nationalist standards prohibiting <u>their definition</u> of adult entertainment/pornography would challenge decades of free speech precedent.

Courts, including the Supreme Court, have long held that adult entertainment is protected by the First Amendment so long as children are not involved and it is not obscene as defined by the Miller test.

Once free speech is restricted, it's difficult to get it back.

"The only difference between death and taxes is that death doesn't get worse every time Congress meets."

~Will Rogers

Taxes

Each year, the IRS makes updates to common tax provisions, such as the standard deduction, to ensure that certain parts of the tax code keep up with inflation.

Making the extreme changes to the tax code that Project 2025 is proposing requires Congressional approval. To prevent future administrations from undoing it, they propose a change in the rules after the new tax code is passed: *"Treasury should support legislation instituting a three-fifths vote threshold in the U.S. House and the Senate to raise income or corporate tax rates to create a wall of protection for the new rate structure."*

The proposed tax changes significantly impacting the middle class, combined with the proposed Consumer taxes, is a recipe for an economic collapse of epic proportions.

It's basic **Economics 101**: The average family will have significantly less money and will buy less—which means companies will sell less—which means layoffs—which means more people will be unemployed and have less money to spend—causing companies to go out of business—creating a huge Federal budget deficit. The definition of a Depression: A DRAMATIC AND SUSTAINED DOWNTURN IN ECONOMIC ACTIVITY, WITH SYMPTOMS INCLUDING A SHARP FALL IN ECONOMIC GROWTH, EMPLOYMENT, AND PRODUCTION.

(1) Enact a two-rate individual tax system of 15 percent and 30 percent that eliminates most deductions, credits and exclusions; Reduce the corporate income tax rate to 18 percent.

ANALYSIS: Currently, there are seven individual tax brackets— 10%, 12%, 22%, 24%, 32%, 35% and 37%—with each based on income thresholds.

Those people at the bottom of the current tax brackets would have their taxes raised. Those at the top would have their taxes lowered. Those earning less than $168,000 (the middle class) would pay 15%. Those earning more than that would pay 30%.

The current corporate tax rate is 21%. The corporate income tax rate would be lowered to 18%.

The tax proposals of Project 2025, if enacted, would likely affect every adult in the U.S. by tossing out the nation's long-standing system of multiple tax brackets, which is designed to help lower-income Americans pay a smaller share of their income in federal taxes compared with middle- or high-income workers. This proposal shifts taxes from the wealthy to the middle class, FULL STOP.

Millions of U.S. households would face higher taxes. Currently, the bottom half of American taxpayers, who earn less than $46,000 a year, now pay an effective tax rate of 3.3% vs 15% under the proposed change where there are few to no deductions.

It's estimated that a middle-class family with two children and an annual income of $100,000 would pay between $2,600-$6,600 in ***additional federal income tax****. By comparison, a married couple with two children and earnings of $5 million a year would enjoy a $325,000 tax CUT.*

But corporations would get another bonanza.

(2) Reduce the capital gains tax to 15%.

ANALYSIS: Currently, high-income earners pay a tax of 20% on their capital gains. This is another proposal that benefits only the wealthy, leaving the working class to shoulder the tax burden.

(3) Implement a Federal Consumption (Sales) Tax

ANALYSIS: The GOP claim is that a consumption tax (a Federal sales tax) would be the least economically harmful way to raise federal tax revenues. The reality is that a federal sales tax would cost the average middle class household an additional $3,500 to $6,800 per year.

"Some people live an entire lifetime and wonder if they have ever made a difference in the world. A veteran doesn't have that problem."

~Ronald Reagan

VETERANS/MILITARY

One of the "takeaways" from the Military section in Project 2025 is continual reference to the "serious shortfall in recruitment" within all branches of service.

Although a 2024 survey showed that the U.S. has the smallest active-duty force since 1940, our military is not "weak." America has been, and remains, the world's military superpower. We are the strongest we have been since 1945.

If the proposals under Project 2025 are enacted, the military will lose thousands of highly dedicated, competent, and patriotic service members.

Although men 18-26 are required by law to register for Selective Service, enlisting in the service is purely voluntary. A draft hasn't been instituted in the country since 1973. That being said, there is language in Project 2025 alluding to some kind of mandatory national service for young men if recruitment efforts fall short of what they believe is necessary.,

(1) Rescind all departmental VA clinical policy directives that are "contrary to principles of conservative governance starting with abortion services and gender reassignment surgery."

ANALYSIS: This means that women in the military will be unable to obtain the medical "standard of care" necessary if they become pregnant and have complications. This policy can be expected to discourage women from entering the military.

2) Reverse policies that allow transgender individuals to serve in the military.

ANALYSIS: In May 2014, the Williams Institute published a research brief estimating 15,500 transgender people were serving on active duty or in the Guard/Reserves, and an additional 134,300 transgender people were either veterans or retired from the Guard/Reserves. The American military employs more transgender people than any other organization in the world.

At least a dozen individuals were discharged from the military in the first six months of the Trump administration for being transgender. There is no record of how many others were discharged.

On January 25, 2021, President Biden issued Executive Order 14004, Enabling All Qualified Americans to Serve Their Country in Uniform stating: "It is my conviction as Commander in Chief of the

Armed Forces that gender identity should not be a bar to military service."

On March 31, 2021, the Pentagon announced new policies to take effect April 30. Under the new rules, transgender service members will not be at risk of involuntary discharge and can reenlist. The military will provide support for gender transitions, including medical care and a procedure to change gender marker.

Regarding transgender individuals, Army Chief of Staff General Milley stated:

> *"The United States Army is open to all Americans who meet the standard, regardless of who they are. Embedded within our Constitution is that very principle, that all Americans are free and equal. And we as an Army are sworn to protect and defend that very principle. And we are sworn to even die for that principle. So if we in uniform are willing to die for that principle, then we in uniform should be willing to live by that principle."*

AFTERWORD

America is not perfect. We still have a long way to go before we fully realize the ideals our forefathers dreamed of on March 1, 1781 when the Constitution of the United States was ratified. But, neither are we a "failed nation" or "a country in decline."

In November 1947 Winston Churchill delivered a speech to the U.K. House of Commons.

> *"Many forms of Government have been tried, and will be tried in this world of sin and woe. No one pretends that democracy is perfect or all-wise. Indeed,* ***it has been said that democracy is the worst form of Government except all those other forms that have been tried from time to time;*** *but there is the broad feeling in our country that the people should rule, continuously rule, and that public opinion, expressed by all constitutional means, should shape, guide, and control the actions of Ministers who are their servants and not their masters."*

Democracy is not easy. It's messy. It's too easy to become complacent about our rights, our Constitution, and our way of life. We're convinced our democratic institutions will hold against any autocratic threat, but we saw during the last Trump administration that we CAN lose our freedoms, we CAN lose our rights, and we CAN suffer the same physical and legal attacks on our government as we have seen in other countries.

We, as a country, are at a critical fork in the road—a deciding moment in history when we need to make a choice between taking the more difficult road of fighting for democracy, or giving up and letting it all fall away. This is a decision once wrongly made, that cannot be easily reversed.

May God bless our Democratic Republic and may our flag continue to wave over the land of the free and the home of the brave.

J.L. Wertis

About the Author

J. L. Wertis is a non-fiction author who writes in the genres of current events, philosophy, politics, biography, faith, and family history.

Ms. Wertis did her undergraduate studies in psychology/sociology at the University of Nebraska at Omaha. She has a Bachelor of Science in Computer Information Systems, a Master's Degree in Business Administration, and did her post graduate work in Behavioral Science—a dissertation short of a PhD.

Throughout the years she has maintained an active interest in social psychology, studying how social and political influences, perceptions and interactions affect individual and group behavior. This interest adds depth to her political, genealogical, and historical works.

She is a member of PEN America, a nonprofit that defends the right to expression through the written word, the Association of Professional Genealogists, the National Genealogical Society, and the Daughters of the American Revolution (DAR).

Made in the USA
Monee, IL
04 November 2026

67384263R00075